Under the Big Oak Tree

Under the Big Oak Tree

Poems

Chris Gallant

Copyright © Chris Gallant 2023

———

chrisgallant.ca

———

All rights reserved. No part of this publication may be reproduced, distributed, or transmitted in any form or by any means, without the prior written permission of the author, except in the case of brief quotations embodied in critical reviews and certain other non-commercial uses permitted by copyright law.

Cover Design: Pendulum Ideation Studios
ISBN: 978-1-7381105-0-6

To every brave soldier fighting in the ongoing civil war against self-doubt—today, if only for a day, we celebrate.

Contents

Spring

Pilot	3
Drive Me Crazy	5
April Showers	6
Unlucky Charms	7
Foolish	8
Addiction	9
Blowing Kisses	10
Friends	11
Hi, My Name's Chris	13
Out of the Blue	16
The View	18
Bud Light Blue Eyes	20
Oversized T-Shirt	21
Hoodies	22
In Between the Lines	24
Maybe: Chris	25
Metamorphosis	27

Summer

Writers Room	31
I'm Sorry	33
I Thought About Telling…	34
Lighthouse	36
Titles	37

Let Go	38
Blue	39
For Him	41
For You	42
Matches	44
Take My Hand	46
Come to Bed	47
A Regular Sunday but…	48
V.I.P.	49
When I See You	50
The World	51
For Me	52
I'm Sorry II	53
Haunting	55

Fall

Growth	59
Birthday Lessons	61
Last First Date	64
Falling	65
Big Sweaters, Haunted…	66
The One Rose	67
When I Write You Into…	71
Happy Meal	73
Three Words, Eight Letters	75
When I'm Slow to Text…	79
Secret Worlds	80
Laugh_Track.wav	83
Blanket Castles	85

Can We Get a Dog?	87
Always	89
Breaking News	91
idk what to say	93

Winter

Hiatus	97
Loss	99
Learning	100
Shadow Puppets	101
Tears	102
Not All Heroes…	104
We Finally Talk About…	105
Thunder Buddies	106
Love Languages	108
Mollique's Birthday	110
Joy	115
Privilege	116
Some Things to Know…	118
Down the Aisle	120
Gravity	121
When the Day Comes	123
Renewed	125

Spring

Pilot

I know it's spring when the rain clouds
start throwing kitchen parties again.
I watch the wildflowers come to life,
drunk off the sky's champagne showers,
do you remember dancing in them,
while the song sparrows & spring peepers
serenaded us into a future
that never bloomed.

Drive Me Crazy

My friends warn me about you—
say you're not ready,
say you're not serious,
say it's not that your flags are red,
but checkered,
when you wave goodnight
they see a finish line,
a last time,
say your grand gesture
will be an expiration date.

But I ignore them,
because what's a race,
if not something begging to be won?

April Showers

Write me a poem
before we go to sleep.

Handpick my favourite words
and plant them somewhere
only my eyes can see—

They're flowers to me.

A garden to drink my coffee in
the morning after you leave.

Maybe one morning
you won't leave.

We'll lie in our flower bed
and grow into oak trees.

Unlucky Charms

We argue over the cereal
until our *hearts* are
no longer recognizable.

If only we expressed
what we each wanted
before we poured.

Chris Gallant

Foolish

I guess I'm the
walking contradiction,
because how can I feel both
liberated and imprisoned
every time you say
you want me.

Addiction

Stab me in the back
and I'll bleed a trail of breadcrumbs
to one more chance.

Again.

Blowing Kisses

You stole the oxygen out of my lungs,
whipped it in the air around me,
and yet, in your eyes,
I felt most at peace.

Then you left me
searching for my voice
under the rubble of broken walls.

Maybe they should name the next hurricane
after you.

Friends

They never say, 'I told you so',
they just bring ice cream
to numb the bitter taste you left.

Chris Gallant

Storms don't always know they're the storm. Not at first at least.
They start innocent, with good intentions, to shower
their world with everything it can't grow without,
they just get a little carried away.
Excited. Clumsy. Reckless.
Destructive.
Storms don't
know they're the
storm, until I
see the
ruins

I've left behind.

Hi, My Name's Chris

but my mom,
she still calls me Christopher,
and you might know me as Chris G
from that stint on national TV.
Others have called me
'Cap', Big C, Stretch, and Lanky.

I'm twenty-nine
or thirty,
idk when I've decided to share this.

I'm six foot five with brown hair and a red beard
when the sunlight catches it right.

I like the sun,
even if some days it doesn't like me,
and I like summer days,
but I don't really like birthdays,
or cake,
which is weird because I've always been more comfortable
when things are sugar-coated.

I crave compliments more than I should,
seek validation from strangers
like they're guardian angels
any chance I could.

Some days I wish I could go back to 9 and 3/4s,
where the world seemed so magical.

Chris Gallant

Like I remember pretending to play the clarinet
just to flirt with my crush,
and unlike that clarinet, I blew it,
but I miss the days where people could run through it,
the walls I put up,
like they were paper-thin,
I'd just let them in.

My favourite colour's blue.
My favourite fruit's an orange.
My eyes are green,
the same shade as summer grass
before the fall ruins things.

Some days I'm a leaf on a maple tree,
waiting for the cold to come for me,
staring at the evergreens,
wondering what's the secret
to endure everything 365 days can throw at me.

I'm still learning to brighten rooms
with the light others share with me,
but not sure how often I deserve to be seen.

'Cause too often
I've been lightning to lovers
who wanted to dance in the rain.

Some days I still spend locked in my subconscious,
scribbling *I'm sorry* into air molecules,
hoping they float into the right neighbourhoods.

Under the Big Oak Tree

My stomach said if I can be more honest,
he'd work on being less upset.
He seems to think those two things are codependent,
and I've been working on listening,
so I've asked my ears to hear him out.

Honestly,
I think I believe in true love,
there are just days I wonder if it believes in me.

Out of the Blue

The first time I see your face,
it turns 8pm on a Thursday into a first date,
my heartrate drumming, running,
trying to escape,
'cause the night's barely on the horizon,
and you've already got me at checkmate.

But you don't know that yet.

So, we let fire dance for your gin and tonic,
sparking the conversation about MDs, MTs,
and the neurologic symptoms of how your presence tempts me,
my hand on your bent knee,
your skin up against me,
the drinks, now they're empty,
we stand,
I leaned in and you met me,
and now I know you know just how you affect me.

I whisper,
can I

and your blue eyes let me.

Under the Big Oak Tree

I kiss you—
you taste like a poem
I didn't know I needed to write.

The View

The first time you come to my place,
you taste sweeter than the cider we pop,
we talk about our absurd bird takes
while we perch on top of the cityscape,
you gaze at the view,
I gaze at your pretty face,
it's buying real estate in my memory,
the energy shifts to together we should
probably go inside,
so, you breathe one more breath of fresh air,
and unzip that dress as we stumble down the stairs,
my thumb cradles your neck and fingers grip your hair,
time stops, but I
continue to stare—

Under the Big Oak Tree

I gaze at you—
ask the tip of my tongue
to introduce every emotion
dancing on its taste buds,
but it communicates through touch,

and we're still learning braille.

Chris Gallant

Bud Light Blue Eyes

Your eyes open a world I never knew existed,
your touch the tour guide giving me an all-inclusive visit,
now I search your heart for real estate that's listed,
because suddenly, you're the home I wanna live in,
with your permission, I'd like to enter any area listed as restricted,
unlock the codes to the places you keep encrypted,
and explore the parts of you that no one else has been in.

Oversized T-Shirt

You don't read poetry,
but you're fluent in fashion,
so instead,
I stitch these words to my sleeve,
call them style,
call them art,
call them yours,
when you slip them over your shoulders,
and they whisper you to sleep.

Chris Gallant

Hoodies

You aren't the first time
I wear my heart on my sleeve.
In the past,
I'd take it out
just so I could leave it on the floor when I undressed,
but with you,
it's different.

I like the way you look at it,
make it feel seen.
I like when you touch it,
hold it in your hands,
you're gentle.

So, one day,
I give you my hoodie,
or you steal it,
either way, you bring it home with you,
sleep with it,
keeps you warm,
keeps you company,
keeps me close to you,
you wear it constantly,
and I like the way it looks on you,
then,

idk,
but you stop wearing it.

I think maybe you're just behind on laundry,
but weeks go by.

Under the Big Oak Tree

Until one day,
you say I should have it back.

So, you return my hoodie,
and I leave it on the floor.

It's safer there anyway.

In Between the Lines

I kinda thought you'd be the one,
so did my journal.

Your name etched like a signature on every page,
my main character at the end of every day,
a protagonist,
I thought.

My hand misses writing all the curves in your name.
My voice flat reading back the future we'll never have,
it's the way you wrote yourself out of the story.

So now I wonder,
reading in between your lines—

Was I always written as someone to erase?

Maybe: Chris

does your heart still beat a little faster
when you drive by my street

does the radio occasionally play you
the same memory it plays me

do you still wear my baggy sweater
does it still smell like me

does your pillow still remember
the imprint of my smile

are there shows you can't watch without thinking of me
there's shows I can't watch without thinking of you

do you miss the way I say your name
do you still say mine when you're lonely

I see you deleted our pictures
but what about our playlists

do you feel the bed is too quiet now
does my ghost haunt your silence

I just want to fall asleep again
I just want to fall asleep again

if I texted
would my voice still read it back to you

Chris Gallant

For months
I only swipe left,
using all three of my wishes that somehow
you pop up onto my screen like Jasmine,
only to keep finding myself alone
in the reflection of my phone
sitting on an ordinary carpet,

'cause unlike Aladdin,
I never got
a sequel.

Metamorphosis

I still have the butterflies you gave me,
but they can't fly anymore.
Pressed into the pages of our story,
entangled with the language of how you made me feel,
it was the only way I could save them.
Preserved, they make up a thousand words,
snapshots of the individual moments you gifted each to me.
I wish they could dance again,
but they had their spotlight,
and we had our song.

Summer

Writers Room

I read and read and read
our history on repeat,
desperate to trip over the moment
responsible for pushing me
into the chamber of your sandcastle
I never thought was meant for me.

Dreaming of tracing my
hands over your spine
until your pages
open up for me—

Tell me,
would it be so bad
if we carve our names
into this beach?

I'm Sorry

It's late,
or maybe it's early
but today marks four days straight we made it past 3am.
Talking, texting, today it's together where
our bodies touch and warm one another,
playing blanket while blanket plays our cover.
My heartbeat beats against your back,
and you pull me closer,
fuelling our inner insomniac,
but…

We're just friends.

So I'm sorry
for staring at you a few seconds too long,
for staying up to text you a little bit too long,
that saying something hurts more than saying nothing,
that being with you hurts more than being apart,
because my heart needs nothing less than something.

Sorry
I'm scared to tell you,
that the plan changed,
promises broke,
and feelings rearranged.

Sorry
I accidentally fell for you,

But most sorry
you *don't* feel it too.

Chris Gallant

I Thought About Telling You This Morning

The same way I thought about telling you yesterday
and the day before
and the day before
and the day before
and the day before
and the day before
and the day before
and the day before
and the da—

I just,
I want it to be perfect.

I imagine—

I wouldn't buy you flowers, but I'd show up with a bouquet of cotton candy because I know that's your favourite colour sky—you wouldn't know anything's going on yet. Not until I whisk you away to the swing set, the one we'd watch the sunset before we knew it was romantic. I bet our names are still etched into that plastic. We'd swing around the world, blind to the consequences of falling. This is where you'd start calling my name, asking what we're doing back here today. And clawing through a million layers of self-preservation, my voice would say something stupid like, "I…uh…I just—you fit into me like wine… into a goblet?" And we'd laugh because what the hell is a goblet, but then I'd raid my soul to drag out the contradiction that your mere existence fills me with pure unfiltered joy and bone-crushing existential dread. I know how crazy that makes me sound, but I'd beg you to understand there's nothing rational about us. And I promised myself I'd stop stumbling into good chemistry just to blow it, so dance with me. History is painted with artists who cross lines, so who cares how we first drew it up when our brushstrokes headline galleries. It's in this moment I'd get down one knee, metaphorically, obviously, ask if I can be your everything in the moments you need anything. And as you'd contemplate the gravity of saying yes, fireworks welcome the sky into its night shift, the same way I'd treat you every night, this can be something if you give this thing a chance. C'mon love, let's get on this swing. I'll show you flight, I'll show you fun, I'll show you France. You deserve a Hallmark romance—

Then I learn tonight,
he exists,
and all he did
was DM you
with Heineken hands.

Chris Gallant

Lighthouse

When you volunteered
to be his safe place,
he never told you how much
he loves the open sea.

I bet being his lighthouse is lonely.

Titles

You
dream of being his everything,
settle for being his anything,
and wonder why he doesn't call you
his
something.

Let Go

He tells you,
scars are just tattoos that choose you.

So even when
hanging on to his every word
means gripping broken promises,
you convince yourself
your hands are a canvas
and they're bleeding art.

Blue

The colour nitrogen and oxygen make while
dressed in beautiful white light,
dancing together,
moments before the clouds roll in
and change the song.

Blue,
your skin after he takes
your coat,
your tuque,
your life away,
then leaves you outside on a rainy day.

Blue,
the ocean of doubt he makes you walk the plank into.

Blue,
his eyes you study like a court case,
and you're his attorney now.

Blue,
the jeans he says makes you look like a broken vow.

Blue,
the jay in the morning windowsill,
listening to him serenade you into a million broken records.

Blue,
the berries you choke down
to chase the bitter taste of disappointment.

Blue,
one shade away from the grass is greener,
yet one more punchline from a purple heart.

Blue,
the hue he paints your world with,
even if he never intended to.

Blue,
is the most loved colour in the entire world.
I'm sorry he didn't make you feel that way too.

For Him

You tossed out honey,
complaining,
the jar was sticky.

But to the bee,
that was everything,
her entire life's work.

For You

You spend your whole life avoiding mirrors,
when all they're begging to do
is convince you
you're someone worth seeing.

Under the Big Oak Tree

*I think of all the poems
waiting impatiently
for me
to give them permission
to write themselves.*

Matches

I'm sorry he never cheered
when you shined.

But that's why
I get a little excited
when God strikes a new match.
I think lighting up this world
deserves a round of applause,
and I promise I'll always
be the thunder to your lightning,
the Clyde to your Bonnie,
taking everything
he was never *bad* enough to take.

Like your breath away.
On rainy days.

Under the Big Oak Tree

You say
'everything happens for a reason'
so let me be
everything,
and you can be
the reason.

Chris Gallant

Take My Hand

Let's dance on all your shattered expectations until your feet are so calloused his disappointment can't hurt you anymore.

Let's pour lighter fluid on the bridge he built to you and ignite it with the candles he lit for her birthday.

Let's burn the letters you wrote for him, and the blank pages he returned to you.

Let's dig up your self-esteem he buried beneath the skeletons you found in his closet.

Let's graffiti all the white lies he painted your colourful walls with.

Let's hitch his memory to a rocket and watch it disappear into space, he doesn't deserve one more molecule of your oxygen.

Take my hand,
let's fill all the empty promises he gifted you.

Come to Bed

Dress in your finest birthday suit,
I made a reservation for two.

Leave your troubles at the foot of the bed,
the monster underneath will take care of them.

Ditch your stress somewhere
in the maze of tangled sheets,
and allow your wildest dreams
to hunt as lions do wildebeests,
until all that's left is
you and me,
lost in time and space,
in the white noise
of this black room,
where we speak
our secret language fluently.

Allow me to be
your weighted blanket,
holding you down tonight.

A Regular Sunday with Your Person, but Make It Spicy

It's dark, or maybe it's light, 11am or 11 at night, I don't know, my watch doesn't work but that's ok because any moment I get with you, that's when time is right. You call my name. Secretly the only combination of letters you need to say to light up every corridor of my brain, I say yes, which room you want me in today? In my head I hope you take that the right way. Now you guide me down the hallway, we talk about something or nothing, maybe I ask about your day, you ask my day, but to be honest I forgot to listen cause I'm too busy breathing in your presence the whole way, you stand in the doorway. Tell me to come in. But speak only with the flirtatious voice who smiles in your eyes. I like her. *I like when she whispers to me.* I listen when she motions me towards you. I tiptoe closer, encouraging tension to have another glass of wine until I'm in your space and you're in mine. I walk in, feel you, next to me, it's ecstasy, I pretend to be unfazed, but what do you expect from me? You have no idea the way you're affecting me, I take a seat, the chair rescues me, 'cause I'm tipsy off the intoxication of your energy, now you start to walk to m—[redacted]

V.I.P.

It's when you see her face in a crowd full of people
and you lock eyes,
shutting out all the sound around you,
and now slow motions all that surrounds you,
and for a second, you're the only two people with an invitation to a
secret concert.

That's when you know.
That's her.
That's the one you shouldn't let go.

Chris Gallant

When I See You

I see bumblebees and apple trees,
the sun flirting with an autumn breeze.

I see a glass so full we could swim forever in it,
a candle dancing even when it's cold out.

I see a smile sparked by a commitment
that we'll never burn out.

I see tattooed memories of lavender sunsets,
dancing under burgundy moonlight,
painting our world the colours we want it to be.

I see the way you look at me,
your eyes, they whisper and wait.

I see your name with real estate on my tongue.
I wanna kiss you into tomorrow,
**** you into yesterday,
and hold you until time stands still.

I wish time knew how to stand still.

I saw bumblebees and apple trees,
the sun flirting with an autumn breeze.

I saw a glass so full we could swim forever in it,
a candle dancing even when it's cold out.

I saw a smile sparked by a commitment,
but sometimes things burn out.

The World

It was my fault,
the way we ended.

I was
so distracted by everything I couldn't offer,
so busy fighting with what I didn't have,
so defeated by what I thought you deserved,
I never stopped to realize
you never asked for the world.

Just a piece of mine.

Chris Gallant

For Me

You spoke her into rain clouds,
and she showered your world
with daffodils and dandelions.

You never deserved her.

I'm Sorry II

Sorry
for smiling because you smiled,
for laughing because you laughed,
for haunting you with compliments,
for promising sunrise,
for sleeping in,
for speaking you into more than friends.

Sorry
I told you,
that the plan changed,
promises broke,
and feelings rearranged,

Sorry
I accidentally fell for you,

But most sorry
you *did* feel it too.

Chris Gallant

*I'm wrong more often than I'm right,
but if there's one thing I do know—*

> *When it comes to
> heroes and villains,
> you don't get to decide
> which one
> others see in your eyes.*

*I'm sorry my only superpower
was drawing lines in sand.*

Haunting

I lock all our *what ifs*
in a safe at the back of my closet,
behind the boxes of memories,
behind our dirty laundry,
behind my skeletons,
because I rather the past haunt me,
than an army
of a million futures, angry
they died too young.

Fall

Growth

Do you remember
sitting under the big oak trees,
with all the acorns
who left home to fulfil their dreams
of one day growing into someone
who makes their parents proud.

Do you wonder
how we're doing, too.

Birthday Lessons

1. Crying gets me what I want.
2. These teeth better be worth it.
3. Kermit is perfect and I wanna be friends with Clifford. But Big Bird is terrifying.
4. Even though I don't care to share, apparently sharing is caring.
5. I hate naps, and bedtime, and healthy food, and showers, and medicine, and especially having nothing to do.
6. Crying no longer gets me what I want.
7. Speaking of crying, I got L'Oréal Kids in my eyes, and they lied, cause I'm bawling and my eyes are sore.
8. Never start with Bulbasaur.
9. Avril Lavigne will go down as the greatest singer of our generation.
10. After nights of sleepless manifestation, practice, self-belief, and determination, after much deliberation, thought, and consideration, I think I've come to the realization that I might be able to go pro in Heads Up 7 Up.
11. Girls are scary & Bill Nye the Science Guy is that dude.
12. Just because someone says 'I love you' in their MSN name, followed by 'forever and always', doesn't mean you'll actually talk in the hallways.
13. But I bet if I make a note on Facebook and cryptically reference one of my six crushes they'll look, and we'll date for short five days and high five once.
14. I think I broke the world record for Brick Breaker on Blackberry Pearl, just trying to ya know, impress my new girl.
15. Puberty stinks. Literally.

16. I figured it'd be more sweet, I mean after watching all those movies I thought I'd have a party, with a platter of charcuterie, with blue cheese, I'd invite 300 of my closest groupies, turn up like a brewery, share cooties, shake booties, dress in dresses and suits, not blue jeans, and they'd all look like they're in their mid-twenties. But instead, I just went *to* the movies.
17. Mac Miller drops Best Day Ever.
Seventeen Again: because sometimes you wish you could live things twice.
18. Sex is dope.
19. They say I need every textbook, yeah I'll buy it. New too, just in case one page is lost in an older edition, no matter what it costs, because you can't put a price on knowledge acquisition. Furthermore, blah blah blah...
20. I've come to the decision— love is real. But I think the first time at least, you only know that when it's over.
21. Is a lot cooler of an age if you live in the US of A.
22. I DMd Selena Gomez the other day 'cause quote, "you miss 100% of the shots you don't take - Wayne Gretzky", Michael Scott. I still missed.
23. As long as you go to the first class, the test class, and the last class, you can skip class and you'll pass with a 'B-'. Also, group work sucks.
24. I love naps, and bedtime, and healthy food, and showers, and medicine, and especially having nothing to do.
25. Why is rent so expensive?
26. It didn't get cheaper.
27. A worldwide masquerade ball isn't as fun as you'd think.
28. I should've bought daisies.
29. Everyone's having babies. Getting married. It's crazy. These days seem to be leaving me behind, and it's scary to believe in Patience when she's always late to tell you if you were right to.
30. Almost as scary as Big Bird.

Under the Big Oak Tree

To be clear,
my biggest fear isn't Big Bird.

Or snakes,
even if that's what my lips sell you
to slink out of the question.

But it's hard to write about love
when love hasn't been writing about you.

That's why I lie.
It's easier to fear snakes.
I'd rather fear snakes.

Chris Gallant

Last First Date

Maybe this is the one,
I show up,
you show up,
and so does Forever,

five minutes late,
like they've just been nervous to meet us too.

Falling

On a blanket
stitched from threads we've yet to unravel,
we watch the sky paint white clouds with golden hour,
play charades with each as they pass by,
sit in grass colour matching your nails,
plant those flags in mine,
and sink into me,
until we flicker
under the candlelight of distant galaxies,
auditioning to be
your memory foam,
lullabied to sleep
by the sky's silent symphony.

The stars have been asking
about you,
the clouds too.

And if the universe believes in us,
maybe I can too.

Chris Gallant

Big Sweaters, Haunted Houses & Game Nights

Fall. Known affectionately as spooky szn, hoodie szn, pumpkin spice szn, cuffing szn, but most importantly for dating, game night szn—because you learn a lot about your partner during game nights.

Are they a chips or candy person?
What about wine or beer?
Do they pick card games over board games?
Do they know that's wrong?
What's the dress code?
Do they believe in guac?
Do they block out distractions?
Do they put their phone on silent?
Do they put their phone on airplane mode?
Do they pre-arrange to courier their phone with expedited shipping to arrive back at their place in the morning?
Have they played the game before?
Do they secretly research it before coming?
Do they lie about having played it to gain a competitive advantage?
Can they count cards?
Will they count cards?
Are they willing to completely sever ties for an indefinite amount of time with the people they cherish most in the world to win a round of Crazy 8s?
Do they know that's the single most attractive quality in a significant other?

—you know,
the basics.

The One Rose (When I Say)

When I say you look really good today,
what I really mean is
the way the light captures your essence
paints a picture so priceless in the art gallery
of my memories
that no distraction could ever pay enough
to buy it from me.

When I say I like who I am around you,
I mean we're in kindergarten again,
I'm the maple leaf,
you're the crayon,
and even though the paper between us
is the wall I put up,
with every gentle touch,
you're still able to bring out the best in me.

When I say you're funny,
I mean your infectious laugh is so contagious
I catch that too.

When I say I'm proud of you,
I mean teleport me back to a distant land where
I transform my heart into a megaphone,
blare your accomplishments
so loud in the town square
they get a head start on
building your statue
that'll one day stand there.

When I say I can't get enough of you,
I mean I'm addicted to the way you rest your head on my shoulder,
like it's your forever home.

When I say come over,
I mean now.

When I say you're my number one,
I mean I've always been attracted to shiny things,
so when your heart pulled me in,
I knew what it was made of.

When I say I wanna make love,
I mean grab the craft box 'cause
I'm gonna glue every compliment
I've forgotten to give you
to paper hearts
and hang them from our first kiss to the bedroom.

When I say I like your perfume,
I mean the moment you step into my proximity,
and I breathe your kinetic energy,
it sparks our electricity,
we light up the infinities,
infinite possibilities,
all when you lean into me.

When I say you're sexy,
I mean the way your mind works turns me on like
mmmm.

Under the Big Oak Tree

When I say I could listen to you for hours,
I mean your voice is snow,
and my ears have only ever known rain.

When I say I like the way you say my name,
I mean your voice is Destiny's Child
'cause it's literally music to my ears,
like the melody makes endorphins swim
like dolphins through my bloodstream,
then lingers to narrate every screenplay that plays in my dreams.

When I say there's just something about you
I mean,
you're the one rose
in a field full of daisies,
even when everything else around you
is beautiful,
you still dare to stand out.

When I say I think you're perfect just the way you are,
I mean

it.

Chris Gallant

#1: Clue

You've got a thing for ropes in the study.

lessons learned during fall game nights

When I Write You Into Poems

Sometimes I write you into poems in hopes we get lost in translation,
playing abstract metaphors like melodies on vinyl,
we dance in circles,
down the uncharted curves of words we haven't yet said.
I hand pick you mismatch bouquets of flowery language,
and you carve our names into the garden we replant them in,
which probably means something,
like a symbol,
but I haven't fully thought it out yet
because sometimes,
when I write you into poems,
it's just to spend time with you.

Chris Gallant

#2: Chutes and Ladders

Climb me like monkey bars
and I'll slide into your—

lessons learned during fall game nights

Happy Meal

When you need a pick-me-up,
I can pick you up,
baby you're not even 5'2",
and you know what we're gon' do—

McDonalds.

Chris Gallant

#3: Go Fish

No.

lessons learned during fall game nights

Three Words, Eight Letters

If I said I love you,

I'd want into your mind, your heart,
to play the strings of whatever chords set us apart.
I'd want the way your eyes light the dark,
the spark that illuminates each and every night.
I'd want hindsight to replay the memories of each and every day,
and the way time only makes you more imperfectly perfect.
I'd want to connect with every aspect of your soul,
to respect that the goal has no right path, no expectation,
just the endless possibilities of our imagination.
I'd want to laugh while we **** to Marvin Gaye hits,

'Cause if I said I love you,
it wouldn't be all serious conversations.
I'm here for the spontaneous trips to Vegas,
singing karaoke while we're just a little bit wasted.
I know compliments aren't complicated,
but roasting is the secret ingredient to intimate relations.

If I said I love you,
I'd shower you with GIFs,
like an unhealthy amount from Winnie the Bish,
and obviously a constant stream from The Office.

If I said I love you,
I'd make pancakes in the morning,
coffee without warning,
shower sex while it's pouring,

or we could stay in bed until the world ends from global warming,
which, according to scientists, is basically tomorrow,
so no pressure,
but let's get it together.

If I said I love you,
I'd smile even when you're snoring,
'cause I'm counting all the ways I can poke fun.
I can see it now,
'Chris, staaaahp, you're being annoying.'

If I said I love you,
I'd want the little things to be a little more than little,
for the middle of rush to be something we savour.
I'd brush my hand across your cheek until you waver,
until you're weak in the knee,
until you crave a taste of me,
like Mini Wheats.

Sometimes I'd ruin the mood with a dad joke
just to see if you're still into me
even in the moments you're thinking about killing me.

If I said I love you,
I hope you kiss me,
'cause your lips
taste like confectionary.

And if I said I love you,
you'd know me well enough
that I just used that word because it sounds fancy,
and I'd do anything to impress you.

If I said I love you,
I'd want to undress you,
strip back those layers that you layer as walls,
breathe in every imperfection, every flaw,
ask to see every scar
that carries the story of who you really are.

If I said I love you,
I need you to know I'm giving you unregulated access to my heart,
and that's terrifying.
There's a reason it's hidden in my chest,
locked up in my rib cage,
it's harder to steal that way,
which also makes it harder to break,
'cause the last time someone took it away,
well, there's a reason it takes me a while to say.

If I said I love you,
just know
it's because
I'm in love with you.

Chris Gallant

#4: Monopoly

I'll buy a railroad just to get to you,
and you should definitely manage our money.

lessons learned during fall game nights

When I'm Slow to Text Back

It's because
I'm stapling these receipts to postcards,
mailing every younger version of me
who never believed
I'd ever be worthy
of your kind of love.

Or I was eating.

(Or both)

Secret Worlds

As a kid,

I believed
imaginary friends,
dressed as shadows,
played tag on brick walls
at playgrounds who taught
there were two ways to
fall head over heels.

I believed
anointed knights,
disguised as stuffed animals,
protected blanket forts
from armies of monsters
lurking in the dark.

I believed
Toy Story
was a documentary.

I believed
there were secret worlds,
and I held the directions.

But one day
adolescence ripped the map
out of the open hands of my imagination,
hid it in the deepest levels of my desire to grow up,
and for years, a piece of me searched for it with no luck.

Under the Big Oak Tree

Until
your shadow showed up,
took mine,
led him to see the world through
your eyes,

and I felt like a kid all over again.

Chris Gallant

#5: Catan

You,
you'll march my heart
into uncharted territory,
build a road,
build a town,
build a kingdom,
and me,
I'll raise an army of sheep,
idk,
just in case, I guess.

lessons learned during fall game nights

Laugh_Track.wav

I don't know what I'll name my future kids yet,
but I practice by naming my playlists after those are born,
and I've been told that's not even close.

I daydream about the parent I wanna be,
the kind that spells 'farts' in Alphagetti,
and 'I love you' in between the pauses of bedtime stories.
I wanna sing karaoke in the dining room,
sketch family portraits with broken crayons,
and hang them inside the throne rooms of sandcastles.

I wanna throw a party for the sandman,
then sugar crash from recklessly driving cake into our mouths,
I wanna nap after that.
I wanna draw treasure maps on Lite-Brites leading to golden memories.

I wanna mow mazes into the backyard so complicated we stop for directions at the family tree we lease to the squirrels.
I wanna host talent shows above them in the penthouse we build,
fill the audience with every imaginary friend you know,
and the real ones too.

I wanna camp in the living room,
roast marshmallows on the fireplace,
tell ghost stories in flashlights around the flame,
share tales of brave stuffed animals keeping monsters away.

I wanna play life-sized board games,
blow bubbles so big we get carried away in them.
I wanna show you the world like that,

then be there for you when it pops.

I wanna watch your bedroom walls struggle to babysit the curiosity in your laugh,
always escaping to find me,
where I'll listen to it on repeat,
like it's the only playlist I'll ever need.

Blanket Castles

This is to my future daughter:

When you turn four,
I hope you come to me and shout:

"Daddy, can you help me build a blanket fort?"

And I'll say to you,

Sweetheart, we're going to build a blanket castle,
and it'll be the most beautiful castle,
with stone walls crafted from colouring books,
towers sculpted from bedtime stories,
tiles laid on so many memories
we could dance forever on them,
and a moat I dig long after your head flutters to your pillow
to keep bad guys away from my princess.

But remember, you don't have to be the princess.

I've heard dragons are cool too.

Chris Gallant

#6: Game of Life

We should've wrapped up more than just ropes in that study.

lessons learned during fall game nights

Can We Get a Dog?

Asks my 8-year-old daughter. 'And don't say no yet, okay? I wrote this letter with lots of reasons why you should say yes!'

Dear Mommy and Daddy,

I'd call him Spot, and we could be the bestest friends ever! Spot would always be up for walks and talks, and even when we're feeling down, he'd be up for a treat, like a bucket of ice cream! Mommy, I know you love ice cream! We could go on cool adventures to the countryside or an ocean paradise. And Daddy, even when you're super tired, Spot would do the best puppy eyes. Then he'd always be there after long days, even the ones you lie and say everything's OK.

I asked my teacher, Mrs. J, about dogs, and she has three of them! She says they're her best friends who somehow understand the complexity of empathy. I don't know what that means exactly, but I guess it's about always being there for me. Mrs. J got a little teary when she told me that, but I think she was happy.

Mommy, Daddy, I promise I'll invite Spot to all my tea parties, and we'll play catch together every day. Maybe not when it's raining. I really, really want another best friend. Love you lots!"

I finish reading, kiss her little forehead, and say, 'We'll think about it.' But what she doesn't know—we've been on a waitlist for seven months and just got the call to pick up our 12-week-old puppy in three days.

I think we should name him Spot.

Chris Gallant

#7 That Hammer Thing at Fall Fairs

Strength is absolutely measured by what you bench,
not how high you lift others up.

lessons learned during fall game nights

Always

I vow
my goosebumps
will always
stand up for you.

#8: Mario Kart

I'll drive off a cliff for you,
multiple times,
too many times tbh,
there really should be more guard rails.

lessons learned during fall game nights

Breaking News

The news of his existence
didn't have a grand reveal,
it just stepped forward,
like a word waking from hibernation,
rolling off the tip of your tongue,

like he was sleeping there the whole time too.

Chris Gallant

#9: Operation

You were supposed to be better at handling misplaced hearts.

lesson learned

idk what to say

i know
you're not coming back
but how do i tell my cat
when he still believes in you

Winter

Hiatus

I'm tired
ending as each other's
wind chill.

Loss

One of the hardest things about loss—
the world doesn't stop.

Just yours.

Learning

In life,
when something sad happens,
I'm guilty of sending search parties
to canvas every square inch,
until they find a positive spin,
believing if I don't,
my mind will wander off the sides of question marks
falling into answers it doesn't want,
but
I'm learning
to love broken hearts
too.

Shadow Puppets

Today, I thought about the night
we made puppets with the last rays of sunlight
clawing into the living room,
begging us to save them from the horizon.

I turned into a blue jay,
you wanted to be a butterfly,
guess we should've known then we were
foreshadowing the day one of us
would fly away.

Together, we made something beautiful,
but only on sunny days.

Tears

When I cry,
I try to remind myself
I'm letting sadness play outside
on an otherwise sunny day.

But sometimes,
I still wonder
how many do I need to collect
for the glass to be half full again?

Under the Big Oak Tree

Do you ever gaze at the night sky,
admire the particles of light from distant stars
who've travelled long enough they don't remember
the places they once called home.

Do they remind you too,
that someone cares?

Chris Gallant

Not All Heroes Wear Capes

Mine wears
a purse,
filled with band-aids,
half-eaten granola bars,
and all the patience in the world.

She wears
a gentle reminder to *text me when you get there*.

She wears jewelry in the shape of my accomplishments,
I'm proud of you in her posture,
and spells *anything is possible* in her walk.

When she talks,
you can find little *I love yous* scribbled
into the periods at the end of every sentence.

She wears *I'll be there* in her smile
and *I promise* in her eyes.

Not all heroes wear capes,
but I bet if you stitched together
every memory my mom's saved for me,
she'd give Superman a run for his money.

We Finally Talk About Fight Club

For years
my dad's fought demons in the dark,
but
the bravest thing he's ever done,

let me in his corner.

Thunder Buddies

Let's talk about mental illness, the stigma that the cure is for them to mind their own business—what is this tradition to think mental health's a decision, a choice they choose to live with? And given the real consequences of the reality we live in, why are we living like we earn a commission by ignoring rather than listen?

One in five Canadians are imprisoned in their mind at any given time and although I'm not in that position, it doesn't mean I'm not in line.

Cause by 40, half of us will have suffered. Felt the dark stillness of the illness echo through the empty cells of our body's prison, but ashamed of our hidden condition, too many of us won't ever reach for a lifeline. We'll just deny why we turn a blind eye, survive by a misapplied high, and hide by a nationwide lie that we're all fine.

When we're not.

Imagine this: it's morning, the alarm rings, and for a moment you're fine. But without warning, a wave of worry floods your mind, drowning any positive vibes who thrive in your stream of consciousness. You didn't ask for this, but it's life. For you. 'Cause every sunrise, you rise, and you try to disguise the invisible cloud looming above your eyes, but even tough guys feel too.

So it's nothing new, the cloud follows you everywhere you move. It evaporates your identity and energy at a rapid rate, leaving only empty chambers of self-hate, and just when you think you can escape, it'll precipitate. Rain down like those divided states, and the pain now will feel like a weight weighing you down, drowning 'til the cycle comes back round.

But what's most frightening, is this storm doesn't make a sound. Void of lighting and thunder, the real danger's that you wonder if anyone else can hear, and fear you might scare away anyone near who assumed the you behind the make-up making up your cover didn't suffer. That you lived in a constant season of summer and sunny when all you needed was a thunder buddy.

So let's talk about this stigma, let's talk about this enigma that is this cloud. And let's talk about it loud—

'Cause this type of sickness doesn't care about our age. If we work for minimum wage or for the stock exchange, it doesn't care about occupation. If we pass or fail, it doesn't care about our education. If we're black, white, or anywhere in between, it doesn't care about our pigmentation. Mental illness doesn't do discrimination like humans who swim in hatred, it just picks us. And over time it afflicts us, preys on our weakness, tricks us, hits and kicks us, 'cause it wants to evict us. Make us believe there's only one way to make it leave.

So please, if you're still with me, breathe.

You're not alone.
You're not alone.
You're not alone.

Love Languages

Dad,

I know every extra hour
you've ever worked,
was you saying
I love you.

So know every extra poem
my hands ever write,
will be me saying
I love you too.

Under the Big Oak Tree

*We tattoo our most beautiful memories
in the moments between the expected.*

Mollique's Birthday

You know that feeling when you're excited for a big night out, so you dig through your closet, find that one outfit you haven't worn in a minute, throw it on, high-five yourself in the mirror, reach in the pocket, and find a $20 bill? Suddenly, your first two drinks are free, and it's all you talk about for the rest of the night.

That was *The Bachelorette* experience for me.

This one isn't a poem, but it's about something that changed my life.

It started on a Monday afternoon. I answered a call from an area code I didn't recognize because everyone has their red flags.

They said, 'Is this Chris?' I said, 'Yes, who's asking?' And they introduced themselves as '[Redacted], calling from [You-Know-Where].'

I said, 'Why?'

They hit me back with, 'You applied!'

I said, 'I did not.'

Now it's a mystery. I like mysteries.

They countered with, 'OK... but like, would you like to date Michelle?'

After a few contemplative milliseconds, I said something along the lines of, 'Yes, of course, what do you mean, please pick me, what is happening, I accept.'

We chatted for a few minutes, they informed me they were still interested (nice), and we wrapped the call.

Within seconds, Morgan (my brother's girlfriend and now a great friend of mine) yelled, 'WAS THAT THEM?'

That's when I knew. Turns out, two days prior, she, my sister, and my mom—yes, my mom—decided that I, Christopher Gallant, was lonely. Their solution? Nominate him to date *The Bachelorette*.

And it worked. Well, sort of.

I'm not engaged. I'm not married. I didn't end the show with Michelle. I didn't get a one-on-one. I didn't get a group date rose. I didn't go to Paradise. Michelle didn't fall in love with me. I didn't fall in love with her. I don't even know if she noticed my pants.

But I did find that $20.

The greatest fear in my life is that my dad won't make it to see my future kids grow up. I've never given that worry air to breathe. Always kept it fending for scraps of oxygen locked in the cellar of my insecurities.

The first time I let it feel sunshine?

A birthday party. Mollique's birthday party.

I told you I've never liked birthdays. But this one didn't have cake. No streamers. No guest lists. No no-shows. Just a few men with no phones, no sports, no work, only each other. And free alcohol.

There's a joke in Bachelor Nation about how overused the word 'vulnerable' is. But I get it now. Because I entered the experience believing I was a vulnerable person—that, of course, it's OK for men to be vulnerable. It wasn't until this moment I realized 'in-theory', and 'in-practice' don't drink together enough.

I can't go into any specific details because *contracts* but while dancing to the music in my heart (only place it's not copyrighted), these men helped me work through my fear. Dug so deep I found the well my tears kept recycling into. The root of my problem.

There was always love in my house. Always. I know my dad loves me. My mom loves me. And we've never been the family that was afraid to say those three words. But we have been the family to avoid conflict. To skip over the difficult conversations. Rather than vocalize, we let feelings drown in their own cries inside a soundproof chamber.

And it was never something we did on purpose. It's just what it was. No one meant any harm. We just couldn't hear the screams inside of us. To do something. To SAY something.

But on Mollique's birthday, I reached into my pocket and found my voice.

When my time on the show was up. When the cameras stopped watching, and the microphones stopped listening. When accountability wasn't scribbled in the fine print of being followed. It was the friendships that kept me motivated.

I returned home, and Casey held me to my word.

I had the tough conversation with my dad. I told him I loved him. I told him what scares me. And I'll be forever grateful for Mollique's birthday for the gift it gave me.

I went on Reality TV ready for love. Truthfully. For marriage. For the next relationship I started to be the one that wouldn't have to end.

Instead, I found $20.

And it's all I've talked about ever since.

Chris Gallant

*Now I know
how many I needed
to feel half full again.*

Joy

Tonight, you can find me
with Joy.
She likes poems,
Joy does,
and penguins, palm trees, and PJ parties.
She likes postcards and planets, pickles and pancakes.
She likes putting pieces of puzzles together.

She also likes unplanned dates.

She's beautiful,
dressed in tomorrow's sunlight,
a walking chandelier,
a touch releasing every compliment the world never thought you
needed to hear.

I can't believe she's flirting with me.

Suddenly, I'm falling deep,
picturing all the places she takes me,
but for once,
something stops me,
says this time, let's take things slowly.

So, at the end,
I just smile and ask,

"Would you like to,
idk maybe,
do this again sometime?"

Chris Gallant

Privilege

For me,

My keys are just keys,
not armour to protect me.

My skin isn't the first thing you see in me.

There are no chemical weapons
deployed in the civil war in my head.

All my ends have always met,
and I've never worried about them getting along.

My heart's never felt the need to hide
the person it wants to ask to dance.

My height's never felt the need to lie,
just for someone to give it a chance.

The name on my resumé feels that way too.

I'm proud now of how many days I wake up,
wander the hallways of the word 'happy,'
but I always remind myself,
it's not hard to find a way in,
when every door's already open.

Under the Big Oak Tree

*Out there
somewhere
someday
I believe
you'll float
into my life
clumsy
but softly
like a snowflake
landing on the
tip of my tongue
melting
into every dream
I've never been able
to put
into words.*

Chris Gallant

Some Things to Know About Loving Me

1. Sometimes when I say I don't want the last slice of pizza, I'm lying. Most times, tbh.

2. My heart loves to soak in sunshine while resting on my sleeve, but often forgets sunscreen. It's been burned a few times for loving recklessly.

3. I have a history of not saying everything I mean. Sometimes my compliments are icebergs, sinking relationships with what's left unseen. And I don't want you to be my Titanic.

4. I can be a little bit of a hopeless romantic. On sunny days, it's kitchen dancing in the spotlight of golden hour. And on cloudy ones, I make it rain your favourite flower.

5. But I think you should know I haven't always had the best luck with roses.

6. I've developed trust issues from things outside of my control, cancelling the love stories I've fallen for.

7. Yes, I do have Netflix.

8. There's no monster under my bed anymore, but by now you know I have a few skeletons haunting my closet.

9. I suppose I hope you have some too.

10. I can't promise you every day will be a helium balloon, but I swear I'll carve the words *I love you* into every evergreen you see walking down the street. I'll tattoo those eight letters into the tire swing hanging off your parents' old maple tree. I'll kiss them into every goodnight before you go to sleep. I'll whisper them into apologies on nights you're mad at me. I'll staple them to infinity each time you look at me. I'll stick them to the sunrise on post-it notes, so in the morning, it's the first thing you see. If you're going to love me, know the studio hasn't given up on me. My writers room is still busy with possibilities, and after sitting in on the latest table read, I think they're ready for their final lead. What I'm trying to say is I'm ready to love you if you're ready to love me.

Down the Aisle

I'm thankful one day
I'll walk down the aisle,

of a grocery store,
with someone who makes it fun and worthwhile.

I'm thankful for the muscles that make us smile,
you know the ones we work out
by lifting our spirits.

I'm thankful for rainy days with a great book,
dog videos on Facebook,
and even though I think it's imperfect
I'm thankful for the way my face looks.

I'm thankful for hobbies,
for a sense of taste,
for literally whoever created copy and paste.

I'm thankful for foggy days,
'cause some days,
I like when my head's in the clouds.

I'm thankful one day
I will walk down the aisle,
wearing a tux, a ring

& you on my smile.

Gravity

I think growing up, I always thought
love is meeting that person on a first date over cheesecake
you wanna ride with, ring up, and root for,
get down on one knee in a suit for,
but I've also learned love
is the subtle escape of laughter
on the day when your heart breaks.

Because love is complex,
and abstract, but enchanting.
Love is nature's way of dancing,
in sync to the rhythm of a heartbeat.
Love is the party,
it draws us in like pencils in stencils.

But love isn't something you see,
so maybe love is gravity,
keeping us grounded to each other
even when our worlds spin recklessly.

Love is poetry of the senses,
emotions flowing together like dresses in the wind,
metaphors like guesses calling you in,
but love can also be simple, like calling your friend.

Love is acting with compassion
even in the presence of rage.
Love is a kingdom, it's not a cage.
Love is amazed at the lengths we go
to be a word on someone's next page.
Love is change, even when we're afraid.

Chris Gallant

Love is the air that surrounds you,
comforts and grounds you,
it's the tension that calls you,
invites and draws you,
it's a soft promise that haunts you,
whispering it wants you to stay,
to say everything is and will always be
okay.

When the Day Comes

When
dreams enter syndication,

When
memories retire to their summer homes in the photo albums,

When
rib cages are museums overrun with the moments they've captured,

When
hearts run out of sheet music and lungs sob behind boarded doors
listening to oxygen beg for one last visit,

When
muscles in smiles clock in for their last shift,

When
that day comes,
hopefully we can all say

I'm ready.

Renewed

I know it's spring when the rain clouds
start throwing kitchen parties again.
I watch the wildflowers come to life
drunk off the sky's champagne showers,
I wanna dance in them,
with the song sparrows & spring peepers,
evergreens, maple leaves, and oak trees
beside me in harmony,
serenading
a new season
bursting to bloom.

Acknowledgements

This list is, and will always be incomplete, but I've learned from experience people are often left out when someone's giving flowers. So please know I do appreciate you, it's my editor who doesn't.

Family
Mom and Dad, Leslie & Keith Gallant—I love you. Thank you for encouraging me to grow into the man I am today, for the freedom to explore passions in places you didn't expect. It's your unconditional love and support that gives me the courage to release this.

To my brother, Josh—You're the world to me, man. For real. We may not have known it back in elementary school, throwing Hot Wheels at each other's heads, but somewhere along the way we became each other's biggest fans, and I'm so thankful for that.

To my sister, Kate—Couldn't ask for a better support system. You've been there through it all, always making sure I stay grounded when things get out of control. Love you for that.

Extended Family
To Morgan Whynot—Thank you for always giving the best advice and opening your brand-new home to me during the pandemic. I can't imagine where I'd be without that year and a half with you and Josh.

To Courtney Gouthro and Robin Lorway at Skills Canada - Nova Scotia—Thank you for trusting me with the freedom to experiment with spoken word poetry in the classrooms while promoting skilled careers to youth. And Shannon Campbell, you organizing my first big performance at the Skills Canada National Competition in

Edmonton in 2018 did more for my confidence and writing than you'll ever know. Thank you for believing in me.

To the rest of my friends who've provided emotional support and reassurance through this writing journey—thank you. That goes for my Skills family, Alexander group, SZN18, and of course, my day ones.

Mentors and Influences
To my fellow poets, specifically Kanaar Bell & Katie Feltmate—you inspire me. Kanaar, I met you six/seven years ago at a slam in Halifax and within 15 seconds of your first poem I knew we had to link. For years now behind the scenes, your drive, passion, creativity, and outlook on life has motivated me to keep with it too. Katie, thank you for being my first audience, all the way back in Creative Writing class at Mount Saint Vincent University. I'll never forget getting my first "Chris, wait… that was amazing!!" from you.

To Rudy Francisco—For years I looked up to you from afar, learning how to perform from watching your videos and reading your poems. Meeting you on *The Bachelorette*, sitting down with you, and then performing with you in the room was a dream come true. I hope I unknowingly inspire new writers the same way you motivated me.

To Tyler Simmons—You might read this thinking, *why am I getting a shoutout?* But Ty, that's just the person you are. The guy who makes others believe in themselves. And this instance was so simple, so small, but you posted under one of my poems 'when's the book coming??' And truly, hearing that from you was the final spark I needed to believe this is something worth doing, that people would want to read what I had to say. I know I'm not the only person you've had an effect like this on, and you deserve every flower tossed your way.

To my exes—If you happen to read this, thank you, and I'm sorry! It's already weird writing stories about real people, about real feelings, emotions, and experiences—the trickiest part though, is the nuance that comes with sharing one side of a story that obviously has two. I tried to leave space for that other side, while staying authentic to my experience and keeping the content as anonymous as possible. I hope I did a good job respecting that, and you.

Readers
And finally, to you, the reader—thank you. Thank you for supporting independent art, for supporting poetry, for supporting me. I hope your next season gives you infinite reasons to smile.

About the Author

Chris Gallant (he/him) is a Canadian spoken word poet based in Halifax, Nova Scotia. With millions of plays across various platforms and captivating live performances in classrooms, colleges, universities, open mics, slams, fundraisers, and a handful of well-known stages, Chris has established himself as a powerful voice in the poetry scene. When he's not writing you can find him with friends and family on the Halifax Waterfront, coaching youth soccer in his community, or cheering on his local pro team, the HFX Wanderers. Chris was also a Reality TV role player (not star).

www.ingramcontent.com/pod-product-compliance
Lightning Source LLC
Chambersburg PA
CBHW031118080526
44587CB00011B/1027